# Monster Trucks

By TORI KOSARA

SCHOLASTIC INC.

New York   Toronto   London   Auckland   Sydney   Mexico City   New Delhi   Hong Kong

Swamp Thing

They have huge wheels. They can pull a car, climb, and jump. They're monster trucks! Monster trucks have bodies that look like regular pickup trucks, but their huge wheels, large engines, and abilities to perform tricks make them monster trucks.

# SAMSON

Most monster trucks put on shows that excite thousands of fans. Monster trucks can jump over and pull smaller cars, climb over other monster trucks, crush old cars, and race each other. Lots of people like to watch monster truck shows.

# RAP ATTACK

The wheels on monster trucks are very tall. They are also deeper than the tires on a car. Most standard car tires have treads that are no deeper than the width of a coin. Most monster trucks' big tires are more than 1.5 feet (0.5 meters) deep!

# KARL MALONE

The average monster truck weighs about 11,000 pounds (4,990 kilograms). Most monster trucks are about 11 feet tall. The tallest monster truck is about 15 feet tall, and weighs in at 38,000 pounds (17,237 kilograms)!

# BIGFOOT

Bigfoot is thought to be the very first monster truck ever made. It is still one of the most popular—and famous—monster trucks in the world. In 1981, Bigfoot became the first monster truck to be in a movie!

# SUPERMAN

It's a bird, it's a plane, it's a monster truck! The monster truck named Superman may not be the comic book legend but it sure has the strength of a superhero when it comes to crushing cars.

# BACKWARDS BOB

Backwards Bob gets its name because the body is placed on backwards! Because the driver's seat faces the back, the truck needs an extra-special design so the driver can see the track.

# DESTROYER

Sometimes monster trucks compete to win prizes at shows. One event at monster truck competitions is called freestyle. The monster trucks perform difficult tricks and stunts. The Destroyer has won several freestyle events.

# BATMAN

The body of this special monster truck looks like the Batmobile from the *Batman* comic books. Batman took home the World Finals Racing Championship, one of the biggest awards for monster trucks, in 2007 and 2008.

EST. 1985

# GRAVE DIGGER

The Grave Digger is famous for mud bogging. In this type of race, monster trucks drive through a pit of mud. The truck that makes it the farthest before getting stuck is the winner.

# MADUSA

This award-winning truck is one of the only monster trucks that is owned by a woman. The title Madusa comes from its owner's professional wrestling name.

# MAXIMUM DESTRUCTION

Monster trucks can fly over rows of smaller cars. Maximum Destruction is famous for its long jumps. But this truck is most famous for performing the first-ever backflip at a monster truck show.

# MONSTER MUTT

Monster Mutt is painted to look like a dog with big floppy ears and a tongue. The truck may look like a harmless mutt, but don't get too close—this monster truck can still easily crush a car.

# BIG DUMMY III

Not all monster truck shows are competitions. Sometimes the trucks perform at exhibition shows. This special event lets monster trucks show off their greatest tricks without keeping score.

# VERVA

Monster truck racing is very popular in the United States. But other countries are joining in the excitement, too. Verva, a monster truck from Poland, is an international favorite that tours in Europe and the United States.

These giant trucks and their cool tricks are sure to excite a crowd. What types of stunts will these awesome vehicles perform next?

# COOL CARS

## BY TORI KOSARA

**SCHOLASTIC INC.**

New York    Toronto    London    Auckland    Sydney    Mexico City    New Delhi    Hong Kong

**F**rom sports cars to supercars, cars come in many shapes and sizes. Some modern automobiles are made for speed and style, while others are using the latest technology to help save the environment.

Race ahead to see some of the coolest cars on the planet!

FORD MUSTANG

# PORSCHE
# BOXSTER

A sports car is meant to be small, easy to handle, and fast—really fast! Many sports cars have big engines that give them the extra power they need to reach high speeds. Some sports cars, like this one, have tops that fold down. This special kind of car is called a convertible.

# FERRARI ENZO

This superfast sports car uses a new technology to help it go even faster. The car's new design and electronic systems will work together to help it be speedier and more powerful during races.

# AUDI
# R8

There are two main types of gasoline: unleaded and diesel. Most modern cars use unleaded gas, but some cars have engines that run on diesel fuel. Some versions of the Audi R8 have a diesel engine option.

# DODGE
## CIRCUIT EV

The Dodge Circuit EV concept car is a sports car that doesn't use any gasoline. Its electronic engine, which runs on a lithium-ion battery pack, can reach speeds up to 120 miles per hour (193 kilometers per hour). The cool design of this car helps it cut through the wind so it can reach its maximum speed.

# FORD MUSTANG

The Ford Mustang is one of the most popular sports cars in America. Over 9 million cars of this classic line have been made. The 2010 model is supposed to look more like the Mustangs that were made in the 1960s.

# DODGE CHALLENGER

This car is a remake of a classic muscle car from the 1970s. But this awesome-looking new version does more than just burn rubber. Unlike the original, this car creates less carbon dioxide, a gas that cars put into the air when they burn fuel.

# LAMBORGHINI GALLARDO

This high-tech car uses new cooling technology in its engine to reach amazing speeds. The Lamborghini Gallardo can reach 62 miles per hour (100 kilometers per hour) in just 3.2 seconds! It can double that speed to 124 miles per hour (200 kilometers per hour) in only 11.8 seconds. Now that's fast!

# SSC ULTIMATE AERO
## BY SHELBY

The SSC Ultimate Aero TT by Shelby SuperCars is the fastest production car in the world. A production car is made at a factory in quantities for anyone to buy it and drive it on a public road. But they still have to obey the speed limit—even though this speedy vehicle can go up to 257 miles per hour (413 kilometers per hour)!

# BUGATTI VEYRON

It might be one of the fastest cars in the world, reaching a top speed of 253 miles per hour (408 kilometers per hour), but it's also one of the most unique. While the Bugatti Veyron is one of the coolest and speediest cars around, only 300 models will ever be made.

Mercedes-Benz
SLR McLaren Stirling Moss
The pinnacle of passion.

# MERCEDES-BENZ
## SLR MCLAREN

The 2009 Mercedes-Benz SLR McLaren might be the most unique car on the road, and that's not just because of the new design that includes doors that open up instead of out, or its ability to reach top speeds. Only 75 of the SLR Stirling Moss edition will cruise the streets.

# DODGE DEMON CONCEPT CAR

A concept car is made to showcase something special about a new type of model, which is made in limited quantities and may never be sold to the public. This Dodge Demon model would be easier to make and more affordable than most concept cars.

# MINI
# COOPER
# CONVERTIBLE

Mini cars have smaller bodies but they can still seat up to five passengers. Mini cars might look small but a large engine is under the hood. That means that cars like this Mini Cooper S Sidewalk Convertible can reach nearly 134 miles per hour (215 kilometers per hour).

# SMART CAR

The Smart car is small and easy to park in crowded places where bigger cars cannot fit. The first model measured 8.2 feet (250 centimeters) long.

Mercedes-Benz is making a new model of the car—an electric car. Electric cars do not need gas to run because they are powered by rechargeable electric batteries.

# FORMULA ONE

Auto racing is an exciting sport to watch! Formula One's Grands Prix and NASCAR's Daytona 500 are some of the most famous car races. Formula One race cars show off the best auto technology in the world.

These cars might be small but they are very powerful. NASCAR's race cars look more like ordinary family vehicles but they can reach speeds of up to 200 miles per hour (322 kilometers per hour)!

# CHEVROLET CAMARO

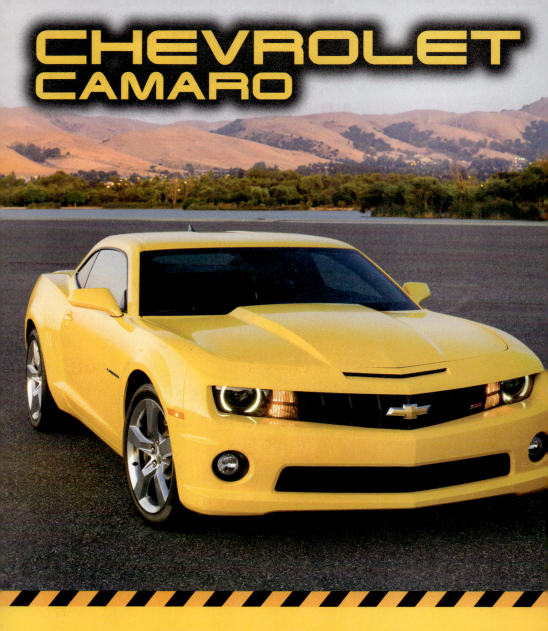

There are a lot of cool cars on the road. What kinds of new models will race into the future?

# COOL CARS

FLIP ME OVER!

Monster Trucks

$ 5.99 U.S.
$7.99 CAN

ISBN: 978-0-545-23333-0

EAN

9 780545 233330

50599

SCHOLASTIC

www.scholastic.com